Love, Di

x

Warmth, wit and wisdom for the
ups and downs of life

DIANNE PARSONS

Care
for the
Family

First published in 2023 by Care for the Family.

Dianne Parsons has asserted her right under the Copyright, Designs and
Patents Act 1988 to be identified as the author of this work.

A catalogue record for this book is available from the British Library.

ISBN: 9781739740733

Design and typesetting by Olive Leaf Design.
Printed in China through Xpedient Print.

Care for the Family is a Christian initiative to strengthen family life, offering support for
everyone.
A registered charity (England and Wales: 1066905; Scotland: SC038497).
A company limited by guarantee no. 3482910.
Registered in England and Wales.
Registered office: Tovey House, Cleppa Park, Newport, NP10 8BA.

Dedication

To all my friends who have shared their
stories with me; those with whom I've
laughed and cried over teas and coffees –
and the occasional prosecco!

Acknowledgements

Writing a book really is a team sport! Special thanks go to Jess Hills for overseeing this project and making this book become a reality. Thanks also to Sarah Rowlands, Esther Holt and Jody Jones. And of course, my love and thanks to my husband Rob, always.

Contents

Introduction

Here we are again; it really does feel like two friends catching up. I enjoyed our time together with *You, Me and Coffee* so much that I couldn't resist the chance to do it for a second time. And if we've not met before, a special welcome. Rather a lot has happened since we last sat down together, not least a global pandemic. In my family, we've faced some really tough days – as you and your family may have too. In the years that have passed since I wrote *You, Me and Coffee* there have been tears, laughter and more ups and downs than I could count.

There's a quote from the film *Forrest Gump* that I really love. The lead character Forrest Gump (played by Tom Hanks) says 'My mama always said life was like a box of chocolates. You never know what you're gonna get.' I don't know about you, but that rings true for my life. We never can predict what is going to happen next. And to be honest, this book follows a very similar pattern! Of course, it's not hazelnut swirls, strawberry cremes or Turkish delights that you'll find here. But what you will find is something that has inspired me, a quote that made me laugh out loud or a small prayer that brought me hope in a challenging time. You may find something that one of our grandchildren asked me, a special excerpt from the Care for the Family archives, or a poignant conversation with a friend that will stay in my memory forever.

Every few chapters you'll find some journal pages and questions for you to consider. These are to help you explore the topics in the book, giving you space to express your own thoughts and feelings.

There may be a storm going on in your life right now or the sun may be shining brightly. Wherever you are and however you are feeling, I hope this book brings encouragement, hope and the occasional smile too. So pull up a chair, make yourself your favourite drink and join me again as we journey and journal together!

Love, Di

x

What Can You Hear?

There is a story of a Masai chief who was invited to New York for a symposium. As he was walking with his host in Times Square, he suddenly stopped and said, 'I can hear crickets.'

His host laughed. 'We can only just hear ourselves speak above the noise of the traffic.'

But the chief insisted that there were crickets nearby and went to a small bush at the edge of the pavement. He fumbled with the leaves for a moment and produced a cricket in his hand. His host was amazed but the chief said, 'It's not difficult. You learn to hear what matters to you. Watch this.' And with that he took a handful of loose change from his pocket and threw it on the pavement. Everybody turned around ...

Words Of Kindness

When I was eight years old, I used to regularly buy a comic magazine called *Princess*. Each Saturday my mum would walk me to the local newsagents to collect it. I would take it home, sit in my nan's old rocking chair and read it for most of the day, and still look through it during the following week. Every month there would be photos selected from pictures sent in for 'Princess of the Month' and she would be surrounded by five other girls, who were runners-up, selected as her maids of honour. I can remember asking my mum if we could send one of my photographs into the comic. I was desperate to be a Princess. I sent one in for the month of May.

May came around and each week, I would hunt to see if this was the week for the Princess to be chosen. Well, the week came when the photographs would appear. As you can imagine I was awake at the crack of dawn and at the door of the paper shop on the dot of nine o'clock. I didn't know whether to go home first or scour the pages there and then. I took the decision to run home as fast as my short legs could manage. My mum was in our tiny kitchen preparing our lunch. She saw my face, rubbed her wet hands on her pinafore and we sat at the table together. Well, there it was … the picture of the May Princess and her 'maids of honour'. My heart sank; I was not the Princess, but I brightened up quickly when I saw my own face looking back from the ring of maids. And there was a prize!

A few weeks later a parcel came to the house. Inside was a pretty silver charm 'maid of honour' bracelet. I was thrilled; I felt so special. The following Saturday I walked around the

corner to a small jeweller's shop. I opened the old wood-and-glass door to the sound of a bell tinkling. From the back came a rather officious man who wore a pair of glasses, attached to which was a small magnifying glass to enable him to see the workings of clocks and watches and to look at precious stones. I was beginning to feel a little nervous under the gaze of this surly gent.

His voice was deep, and like something out of a fairy tale he bent over the counter and asked me what I wanted. I put a little clutch of tissue paper which contained my precious bracelet on the counter, looked up at him timidly and asked him if my prized possession was really silver. He gazed through his microscope for a moment and then threw the bracelet across the counter at me, saying, 'It's lead.'

Was he right? Yes. Was he kind? No. A more tender heart would have said, 'No, my dear, it is not silver, but it is beautiful, and I can see it is very special to you. Guard this precious bracelet well.'

Many years have gone by since that day, but it is still clear in my mind. Perhaps that shouldn't be a surprise. In fact, the book of Proverbs says that our words actually have the power of life and death.

To be sure, since that day I have toughened up a bit, perhaps become a little more secure, but even so, I'll appreciate it if you remember the power of your words and mingle your honest judgements of me with a little kindness – and I'll try to do the same for you. And once in a while, if I am going out somewhere special and feel a bit nervous about my dress – you can even drop the honesty!

A Mother's Temptation

Kids get so much for Christmas and it's easy to get frustrated when they don't seem satisfied. One mum whose twelve-year-old son was never grateful for any of his presents was tempted just to wrap up batteries with the words 'Toys not included!' Instead, she sat him down and said, 'Son, I want you to realise how blessed you are and to share those blessings with those around you. This year, you can have new toys only if you give away a number of toys you have already to a children's charity'.

A Little Prayer

I am only five feet tall and really struggled at school. I still remember some of the feelings I had at the time because of my diminutive size. Perhaps that's why this prayer caught my attention.

> *Jesus, I am so grateful that it's OK to be little. I don't have to be the sharpest tool in the box, or the loudest voice in the room. I don't have to be the biggest, bravest or the strongest. I don't need to have all the answers. Thank you that all you want is me. Sometimes I feel like the boy who brought his lunch to Jesus – I seem to have so little to give. But as I hand it to you, I can hear you say, 'I can work with that. Just watch.'*

Women's Ads

The other day I walked into a department store and was walking through the cosmetics section. These days I don't tend to be bothered by the salespeople quite as much as I used to be, but for some reason I caught the attention of a very keen assistant who approached me with a smile that I swear was painted on. She said, 'Madam, do you have time for me to have a quick look at your face?' I had already had a good look at that face at 7.15 that morning and found it hard to believe that anybody not blood-related or bound to me in marriage would also want to spend time gazing at it.

'Not now, thank you,' I replied, as if there was a possibility that I would let her do so if only she made an appointment.

'No problem,' she said. 'But take this.' She thrust a free sample of something into my hand.

As I walked away, I gazed down at it. It was some concoction that dealt with 'the problem of wrinkles' and had the word 'miracle' in it. Now, I'm not the most confident person in the world, but even I find it a bit of an insult to suggest that the only thing that can sort my face out is divine intervention.

And anyway, in some ways I have grown fond of those wrinkles. Those lines have been caused by laughing with friends and family and shedding tears for those I've loved and lost. My body has carried and birthed two children who have grown into wonderful people who have become my friends.

Now I'm all for looking as young as I can but somehow, I have had to come to terms with the ageing process and accept it. I once heard a woman being interviewed on the television.

She had explained that her remarkable victory over the ageing process was largely due to the skill of her husband who was a plastic surgeon. After pointing out the many operations she had gone through she said, 'He will never get tired of me, because if he does, he can change me.'

Good luck with that one, sweetie! But on a more serious note, I found that such a sad thing to hear her say. I hope that all of you are blessed with people in your life who love you no matter what you look like.

Today's Forecast:

Unproductive ... with a high
chance of an afternoon nap!

The Doorkeeper

I absolutely love learning about interesting people in history. Some time ago, I came across a beautiful story which was too lovely not to share with you. It was a tale about a man named Alphonsus Rodriguez, who was born in 1533 in Segovia in Spain. He was just a young boy of fourteen when his father died, forcing him to leave his education in order to put the needs of his family first. As I delved into his life more deeply, I discovered what an amazing man he was. Alphonsus was twenty-six years old when he got married, but his young wife sadly died in childbirth five years later. Within a few years both his mother and his son died – in fact, he lost all his children – and it wasn't long after that his business began to fail, and he had to sell it. He then applied to become a Jesuit priest but was refused admission because he wasn't educated.

But here's where the story comes into its own. Alphonsus applied to go to school to learn Latin. Even there he was mocked by others and laughed at by the younger pupils due to his background. In 1571, he was accepted into the Jesuit priesthood and sent to a college in Majorca where he served as a humble doorkeeper for forty-five years. He was never promoted, and he never became the priest he wanted to be, but he turned his role into a calling by God. Each time he heard that doorbell, Alphonsus would say to God, 'I'm coming, Lord', and then he would answer the door and welcome the visitor as if they were Jesus himself.

I would have loved to have rung that bell and been welcomed inside by Alphonsus. As I read his story, I asked myself what it was that had driven this man. He'd faced so many obstacles from such an early age, but he'd kept on pushing through the barriers. He was meek, but meekness should never be mistaken for weakness; Alphonsus made an incredible difference to the lives of hundreds of people. In a world that can be cold and unwelcoming, he offered love and acceptance – he made them feel wanted. I once read that meekness is 'strength under control'. I like that.

As I read his story, I couldn't help but think of that incredible statement of Jesus, 'Behold, I stand at the door and knock, and if anyone opens the door, I will come in and eat with them and they with me.'

I'm sure Alphonsus had many meals with Jesus.

Missing The Music

Life is busy. I know that. Nevertheless, I am often challenged to consider what I am missing by my preoccupation with hurry and getting things done. Here is one of my favourite poems and a story.

What is this life if, full of care,
We have no time to stand and stare?
No time to stand beneath the boughs
And stare as long as sheep or cows:
No time to see, when woods we pass,
Where squirrels hide their nuts in grass:
No time to see, in broad daylight,
Streams full of stars, like skies at night:
No time to turn at Beauty's glance,
And watch her feet, how they can dance:
No time to wait till her mouth can
Enrich that smile her eyes began?
A poor life this if, full of care,
We have no time to stand and stare.

Leisure (1911)
W. H. Davies[1]

It was a cold January morning when a man stopped in a New York subway, bent, undid the clasp on his music case, took out his violin and began to play. The subway was busy, and people rushed all around him as he played his way through six pieces by Johann Bach. For what seemed an age, nobody stopped to listen, but finally a middle-aged man hesitated in his rush through the station, listened for just a few seconds and then hurried on. It was a minute later that the musician received his first tip; a woman threw a dollar bill into his open music case but didn't stop to listen. Shortly after she left, a man lounged against a wall, listened briefly but then looked at his watch and hurried on. He was obviously late for work. The person who paid most attention was a three-year-old boy who stopped and listened in wonder. His mother was in a rush and pulled him along, but he resisted and even as he was being yanked away, he kept looking back at the smiling violinist. He wasn't the only child to react like this. Several other children were dragged away by their parents.

The man played for forty-five minutes and in all, collected thirty-two dollars. Nobody who gave money stopped to listen for very long. When he finished playing, nobody applauded, and when he packed his violin away, nobody yelled 'encore.'

Which was a pity, because the musician was Joshua Bell, one of the finest violinists in the world. The instrument on which he was playing was worth 3.5 million dollars and just two days before, he had played at a sell-out concert in Boston with tickets costing a hundred dollars each.

W. H. Davies was right. We really are poorer when we have no time 'to stand and stare.'

The Job Of A Grandmother

As I write, my nine-year-old granddaughter has come into my study and asked if I would like a cup of tea. Of course, I said yes. When she handed it to me, she said, 'Don't drink it if it's horrible. I won't mind.'

I put my arm around her and pulled her close. 'I'm sure it will be delicious,' I said. I took a sip. 'Wonderful!'

A smile lit up her face. When she had gone, I gazed at the liquid in the cup. It looked as if the teabag had been waved over the water and never actually landed in it. I took another sip: tepid.

Ah, I can almost hear your criticism: 'Unless you're honest with her, she'll never learn.' But you won't change me. Parents are for learning. My role is to swallow milky brown water with five sugars (when I don't take any) and say, 'Magnificent!' After all – I'm a grandmother!

I'll Do It Tomorrow

I like the quirky book of Ecclesiastes in the Bible. It has some fascinating comments in it. I remember the occasion when my son Lloyd was about five years old and he sneaked a Crunchie bar from the cupboard. Unfortunately for him, that wasn't the only sneaking going on. His older sister was quick to tell me of his misdemeanours. When I challenged him, he said, 'How do you know?'

I thought I wouldn't drop his sister in it – in any case the chocolate smeared all over his lips meant I didn't really need to! – so I said, 'A little bird told me.' If you have ever used that little device, you may not be aware of its origin – that old book tucked away at the heart of the Old Testament. It says, 'Do not revile the king [...] because a bird in the sky may carry your words and a bird on the wing may report what you say.'

But it's another verse in that book that really challenges me. You see, I'm a bit of a procrastinator. I love that little phrase 'I'll do it tomorrow', especially if the task is boring. I hate cleaning out my fridge and now that my kids are grown, they tell me off for shelves full of passed 'best before' foods. The other day Katie said, 'Mum! There's penicillin growing in there!' But so often it's not a boring task I put off but something I want to do. It could be a course I'd like to start, a book I really want to read, or somebody that I know I should visit. The only problem is that I am brilliant at coming up with reasons why it may not be a good idea to start right now.

— 'If I sign up for the course today, I may have to miss a session next week if the kids ask me to babysit.'

— 'I'll start that book when we're on holiday; then I can really get into it.'

— 'If I visit Mary today, she might be busy.'

So, what's the verse that challenges me? It's found in Ecclesiastes chapter 11, verse 4: 'Whoever watches the wind will not plant; whoever looks at the clouds will not reap.' In other words, we can always find an excuse not to start something. 'If I plant the seeds now, well, it's sure to get windy and they'll all blow away. If I start the harvest today, I bet it will rain and it will all be ruined.'

I have learnt that the time is rarely perfect to start any task and sometimes you just have to get on with it. Sign up for that course, read the first page of the book, make the visit; just stick that seed in the ground.

I don't want my epitaph to be the same as that of James Albery (1838 – 1889):

He slept beneath the moon,
He basked beneath the sun,
He lived a life of going-to-do
And died with nothing done.

Last At The Cross, First At The Tomb

I love a good crime novel and one of the foremost writers of this genre is Dorothy L. Sayers, perhaps best known for her Lord Peter Wimsey books. But Dorothy was not just a commentator on the evils of life but also on the hope of faith. In one of her essays, she wrote about why women had such a care and love for Jesus; after all, they were the last to leave the cross and the first to visit the tomb.

> *'They had never known a man like this man – there had never been such another. A prophet and teacher who never nagged them, who never flattered or coaxed or patronised; who never made jokes about them, never treated them as 'The women, God help us!' or 'The ladies, God bless them'; who rebuked without querulousness and praised without condescension: who took their questions and arguments seriously, who never mapped out their sphere for them, never urged them to be feminine or jeered at them for being female; who had no axe to grind and no uneasy male dignity to defend; who took them as he found them and was completely unselfconscious.'[2]*

Competition

Are you competitive? Do you want to win a game at all costs, even if you're playing against children? Rob may say that he isn't competitive, but the truth is that he's been known to carry a chair with him when we're playing musical chairs at Christmas.

Over the years I've watched so many races on school sports days. Many of them take it so very seriously! I love to sit back and watch their faces through the race and then at the end. The joy and smugness of the win, and the deep disappointment of the loss. And these are just the parents! I heard recently that some schools have actually banned parent races due to how competitive the parents have become. Can you believe it? But it's not just school races; we see it in the push to get on a train at a busy London underground station, the quickening of our step to get to the counter first at a supermarket, or in our dogged determination not to let that driver into our lane.

I read a really heartwarming story recently. Jacqueline Nytepi Kiplimo was an elite Kenyan athlete competing in the 2010 Zheng-Kai marathon. She had a real chance of winning it. At the 10K mark she was in the lead, but then she saw a disabled Chinese athlete struggling to open his water bottle; he was severely dehydrated. She slowed down to help him and then ran alongside him right up to the 38K mark, helping him to drink at each of the water stations. As she was with him many of her fellow competitors swept by. She finished the race in second place. Shortly after the end of the presentations, a journalist asked her what made her make such a sacrificial decision. I love the simplicity of her reply. 'I do not regret my actions. Imagine if I had not assisted him. Sometimes we need to help out even when competing.'[3]

I'm pretty sure that I will never have the opportunity to give the help that Jacqueline Kiplimo did. In fact, if you're running a marathon and you need help from me, you're probably in more trouble than you think. But I do think that I'll remember Jacqueline when I'm jostling for a seat on a busy bus, or it seems like 'handbags at dawn' over that parking place. Anyway, didn't somebody once say that win or lose, one day there's going to be a bit of a reversal: 'The last shall be first and the first shall be last'? (Matthew 20:16.)

What do you
have that God can
work with?

(A Little Prayer)

What so-called 'imperfections' can you be thankful for?

(Women's Ads)

Who can you
'run alongside'
in this season of
your life?

(Competition)

We learn to hear
what matters to us.
What do you hear?
(What Can You
Hear?)

What have you
been putting off
that you could
start today?

(I'll Do It
Tomorrow)

It's OK
To Cheer . . .

It's OK to cheer for the kids who
come first, but remember to stick
around for those who come last.
They ran the race too.

Lessons Worth Learning

We recently became the owners of the most beautiful, black curly puppy. She is fun, mischievous and naughty and we absolutely love her. Is it like having another child? You bet it is. The fascinating thing is that this little creature has already taught me so many lessons about life.

Some years ago, Rob and I came across the following piece. I loved it when I first read it but since Winnie's arrival, I enjoy it even more.

Things you can learn from a dog

— Never pass up the opportunity to go for a joyride.

— When loved ones come home, always run to greet them.

— When it's in your best interest, practice obedience.

— Let others know when they've invaded your territory.

— Run, romp and play daily.

— Be loyal.

— Never pretend to be something you're not.

— If what you want lies buried, dig until you find it.

— When someone is having a bad day, sit close by and nuzzle them gently.

— Take joy in spending time with friends and show affection.

— Avoid biting when a simple growl will do.

— When you're happy, dance around and wag your entire body.

— No matter how often you're scolded, don't buy into the guilt thing and pout ... run right back and make friends.

— Delight in the simple joy of a long walk.

Winnie – thank you for those helpful lessons. And here's one from me to you: if you poo on my carpet just once more, don't rely too much on the 'run straight back and make friends' thing.

A Sideways Look

I came across this little poem recently and it really made me think …

> *I had a side,*
> *And I thought my side mattered a lot, a lot.*
> *The people on my side*
> *were like me,*
> *and they made it feel good to be like me.*
>
> *What I couldn't see*
> *from my side,*
> *because I was blinded*
> *by my reflection*
> *in all the people on my side*
> *was that I wasn't put on this earth to create sides*
> *or choose sides.*
>
> **Attributed to Tod Jenkins**

Afraid Of The Dark

A little boy was afraid of the dark. One night his mother told him to go out to the back porch and bring her the broom. The little boy turned to his mother and said, 'Mama, I don't want to go out there. It's dark.'

The mother smiled reassuringly at her son. 'You don't have to be afraid of the dark,' she explained. 'Jesus is out there. He'll look after you and protect you.'

The little boy looked at his mother really hard and asked, 'Are you sure he's out there?'

'Yes, I'm sure. He is everywhere, and he is always ready to help you when you need him.'

The little boy thought about that for a minute and then went to the back door and cracked it a little. Peering out into the darkness, he called, 'Jesus? If you're out there, would you please hand me the broom?'

The Challenge Of Change

'There is a time for everything and a season for every activity under the heavens.' (Ecclesiastes 3:1)

Do you find change difficult? I do. Oh, I like to think I am adventurous and up for a new challenge, but especially as I get older, I so often want to just leave things as they are. I don't know about embracing the great changes of life: heck, some days I find the prospect of changing the bedding a challenge. And yet, as the old philosopher of Ecclesiastes reminds us, change is not only vital but inevitable. I pray with all my heart that I don't develop into one of those people who fight anything new with all their hearts – like the woman who said, 'If God had intended us to fly, he wouldn't have given us the railways.'

I heard of a particularly difficult parishioner who, on hearing that the vicar was changing something in the parish, collared him one Sunday and said, 'But Vicar – what if the new idea doesn't work?'

The poor man had obviously had his fill of her over the years. 'No problem, Mrs. Davies,' he replied wearily. 'If the new idea doesn't work, we'll just go back to what wasn't working before.'

An Interview With God

I dreamed I had an interview with God.

'So you would like to interview me?' God asked and smiled.
'My time is eternity. What questions do you have for me?'

'What surprises you about humankind?' I asked.

God answered,
'That they get bored with childhood.
They rush to grow up, then long to be children again.
That they lose their health to make money,
and then lose their money to restore their health.
That by thinking anxiously about their future,
they forget the present, such that they live in neither the
present nor the future.
That they live as if they will never die,
and die as though they had never lived.'

God's hand took mine and we were silent for a while.

And then I asked,
'As a parent, what are some of life's lessons you want your
children to learn?'

'I want them to learn they cannot make anyone love them.
All they can do is let themselves be loved.

To learn that it is not good for them to compare themselves with others.
To learn that it only takes seconds to hurt someone they love, but it can take years to heal.
To learn that there are people who love them dearly, but simply don't know how to express their feelings.
To learn that two people can look at the same things, but see them differently.
To learn that it is not enough to forgive each other, but they must also forgive themselves.'

'Thank you for your time,' I said humbly.
'Is there anything else you would like your children to know?'

God smiled and said,
'Just that I am here … always.'

Author unknown

Do What You Can

I absolutely love the Wimbledon tennis tournament. I'm normally glued to the television, but on a couple of occasions I've been fortunate to go with a friend who managed to get some tickets. The buzz of excitement when you enter those hallowed gates is palpable, and I'm a little ashamed to tell you that whenever I've seen anyone famous walk past, I've become a bit teenager-ish! I've walked past the 'You cannot be serious' John McEnroe, the very tall Boris Becker… (I won't continue in case you think I'm name-dropping – Sampras told me that was wrong!). Mind you, a word of advice if you are able to go – do take your own food and tipple, as not only is it very expensive, but it's possible to miss a good chunk of the action while you are queuing! I have to say, I loved watching the golden oldies playing. People like Björn Borg, Jimmy Connors, Evonne Goolagong, John Newcombe, Andre Agassi and others. I loved the entertainment they brought to the court, especially Nastasi and Newcombe. It was so much fun.

There was one player who made a big impact on me in years gone by. His name was Arthur Ashe. He was the first, and still is the only, black American man to win a Wimbledon final. He went on to win many other titles, but what caught my attention with this particular young player was his sheer grit and determination. He suffered very bad health and had a number of heart operations. During one of those operations, he was given a blood transfusion which was contaminated with the HIV virus. It was during that time, before his death in 1993, that Arthur poured himself into raising awareness about

AIDS. He spoke at the United Nations and laid the groundwork for a five million dollar fundraising campaign.

Below is one of my favourite quotes of his.

> *'Start where you are.*
> *Use what you have.*
> *Do what you can.'*

If . . .

I mentioned Wimbledon a moment ago, and that wonderfully encouraging quote from Arthur Ashe. But there is another quote that challenges me. It is written over the archway that the players have to pass under as they walk onto and off the centre court, and it's from the poem 'If' by Rudyard Kipling:

> *'If you can meet with triumph or disaster and treat those two imposters just the same …'*

When I was young I could never understand that quote, but the years have taught me that my successes are very often not quite so lined with silver as I first thought, and thankfully my apparent failures are often not quite so terminal.

My New
Workout

'I started a new exercise routine.
Every day I do diddly-squat.'

Decision Time

Here's one to try on some of the children in your life.

Three frogs are sat on a stone.
Two decided to get off.
How many were left?

Unless the kids in your life are mini Einsteins, with a bit of luck they'll scream out 'One!'

But of course, the answer is three.

Because deciding to do something and actually doing it are quite different.

PS I have decided to join a Pilates class and give up chocolate …

A Bride Remembers

After thirty-six years of living in our current home we are moving, and I have finally decided to put some time aside to declutter! I have to admit that even the thought of doing it has brought me out in a cold sweat. There are two things that you need to know about me. The first is that while I am by no means a hoarder, I do love to keep special things given to me by my friends and family – especially the grandchildren. The second is that when I start to empty drawers that are full of 'stuff', I'm very likely to discover things that I haven't seen for many years. You'll then find me sitting and dwelling on all of the memories that they bring to mind. Needless to say, this won't be a quick job!

The first things that I've come across are some of our 50th wedding anniversary cards. Fifty years – I can't quite believe it. Instead of throwing them away immediately, I decided to sit and look through them. And as I did, my mind couldn't help but wander back to our wedding day. I can't always remember what I had for breakfast, but I can remember that day as if it were yesterday. I felt like a million dollars and Rob looked like a film star (he still thinks he does even now!).

And I remember our honeymoon. We went to the Costa Del Sol for eleven days, full board, including flights for thirty-five pounds each! Before you express wonder at what great value it was, let me tell you that it wasn't very long into the trip that I thought it might have been on the expensive side. The plane was delayed, and we spent our 'honeymoon night' in the lounge at Stanstead airport. We obviously weren't the

only ones to have that privilege. I will never forget the sight of people wandering around, totally shattered, some still in their wedding outfits – one man in a morning suit with a wilted carnation in the buttonhole.

But even so, nothing could quell our excitement. Rob and I had only been abroad once before, and the vision of nights of passion underneath a Spanish sky was enough to keep our spirits up. We achieved fifty percent of that. We were indeed under a Spanish sky, but the nights of passion were exceedingly thin on the ground.

To say we were inexperienced sexually would be to put it mildly. The truth is, we didn't have a clue. Worse still, a very well-meaning but not very bright older couple at our church had warned us while we were teenagers of several dangers that could occur in 'sexual intercourse'. They made those two words sound like 'serial killer' and were no doubt trying, in their words, to 'keep us pure.' They warned us darkly that, 'In the act of sexual intercourse it is possible to 'get locked.'

We were fifteen and my eyes were wide at this prospect. I said, 'What do you mean 'locked'?'

The husband didn't elaborate, just repeated the warning, 'Well, it's possible to get locked.'

I asked, 'What would happen if we … got locked?'

He looked at us triumphantly. 'You'd have to go to the hospital to be unlocked.'

I can tell you that the thought of Rob and I sidling down the road towards the Cardiff Royal Infirmary was enough to keep me 'pure' for a lifetime – and almost did.

The truth is that even by the time we were married we didn't have much idea what the sex side was all about. I realise how quaint that may sound now. But finally, we slid into bed with great anticipation that the ground might move. It did. But only because the builders next door, having had their siesta, went back to work with renewed vigour.

By ten o'clock I really did have a headache, brought on not just by the noise next door but the lingering doubt that the old couple might be right, and Rob and I would be in a Spanish medical centre being separated before the night was over. Finally, after much fumbling and sighing we both fell asleep exhausted. But at least we were nowhere near becoming locked!

A Little Advice To My Younger Self

Life has taught me lots of lessons, some of which you'll find in this book. Someone recently asked me if there was anything I wish I could say to my younger self. Here's what I came up with.

1. Don't try to be anyone else but yourself.
2. Don't judge others – you may never know what they're going through.
3. You don't need to prove yourself to anybody.
4. Be someone who encourages those around you.
5. Choose friends who lift you up, not bring you down.
6. Read as much as you can – it's good for the imagination and for conversations too.
7. Take time out when possible. Rest is not a bad thing.
8. Be generous – share what you have.
9. There is always light to be found, even in the darkest of times. Have hope.
10. Don't be surprised if one day you wake up and realise that you've become your mother, despite vowing that you never would.

Is there anything that you'd add for yourself?

Somebody asked me recently, 'If you could live your life over again, what would you do differently?' It really got me thinking and as I pondered, I concluded that I'd try hard not to take things for granted – perhaps try to worry a bit less (I can be a bit like Mr Worry in the *Mr. Men* books!) and to live in the moment a bit more. I was challenged by these words from an elderly woman: 'I've had a wonderful life. I just wish I'd realised it sooner.'

An old woman looked back on her life and considered how she would do it differently if she could turn the clock back. Here's some of what she said:

> 'If I had my life over again, I would limber up. I would be sillier than I have been on this trip. I would watch more sunsets. I would do more walking and looking. I would eat more ice cream and less beans. I would have more actual troubles and fewer imaginary ones.
>
> You see, I am one of those people who lives life sensibly hour after hour, day after day. I've been one of those people who never go anywhere without a thermometer, a hot water bottle, a gargle, a raincoat, an aspirin and a parachute.
>
> If I could do it over again, I wouldn't make such good grades except by accident. I would ride on more merry-go-rounds.
>
> I would pick more daisies.'

Nadine Stair, aged 85[4]

I think Nadine and I would have got along just fine.

It's A Disease

Somebody once said that the problem with parenting is that by the time you get the hang of it, you're redundant. As I look back, one of the things I wish I'd learned much earlier is not to feel so guilty all the time.

It's a disease that's especially prevalent among mothers. You'll recognise the symptoms when you hear phrases such as: 'I'm sorry, but ...' or 'I know I ought to, but ...' If you ask a mother if she goes out to work, she might reply, 'No, I'm just at home with the children,' or perhaps, 'Yes, I do work – but it's only part-time, and she really loves going to the childminder, and I'm always back for bedtime, and we have quality time together when I'm not at work ...'

The disease is called guilt. We sufferers feel the need to justify ourselves to others, to apologise for our actions, and to constantly compare our own shortcomings to those of other people. It starts when you're a mum-to-be. You feel you shouldn't have had that cup of coffee/run for the bus/painted the bedroom ceiling on your own – because it might be bad for the baby. But the guilt reaches its antenatal height in the delivery room. Some of us might even feel that we 'should' be able to manage without gas and air/pethidine/an epidural. I tried it – for thirty seconds!

After the birth it gets worse. Your baby is the only one in the hospital who cries through the night and keeps everyone else awake. You know you ought to breastfeed, but you simply can't. You 'must' have your washing-up done and be out of your dressing gown before the health visitor arrives at 10am.

And so, it goes on. The guilt grows with the child, reaching peaks when everybody else's child is potty-trained first and seems to reach all the other milestones earlier too. You should have put her name down earlier for that really good school – now her whole future career is spoilt because you were too late. You should have been there for sports day – even though it was your grandmother's funeral that afternoon. You should have noticed it wasn't just teenage angst and wanting time off school – it was actually glandular fever.

You feel guilty because you leave your child and go out to work while the woman next door is a stay-at-home mum. What you don't realise is that the woman next door is feeling guilty that she isn't earning money for the family, because she is home with pre-schoolers all day. And she's feeling inadequate because she watches how well you seem to cope with balancing career and family!

Why can't we decide what's right for us as a family, and go ahead and do it – whether it's breastfeeding, going back to work, moving house, having another child – without worrying so much?

I wish I hadn't been such a sucker for guilt. After all, there is no one way to be a perfect parent, but there are a hundred ways to be a great one.

If you could
interview God,
what would you
ask him?

(An Interview
With God)

53

What advice would you give to your younger self?

(A Little Advice To My Younger Self)

What has guilt
made you believe?
How can you
combat it?

(It's A Disease)

What is one lesson
that you've learned
so far in life?
(Lessons Worth
Learning)

59

What things,
big or small,
can you do?

(Do What You Can)

Looking For Trouble

Sometimes we make life more complicated than it needs to be.

Some years ago, I knew a primary school teacher. One day, a psychologist visited her class and asked to examine the children's artwork. As you can imagine, it was pretty varied! One little boy had drawn everything in black – black trees, black clouds, black grass, black everything.

The psychologist said to the teacher 'Look at this child's drawing. It could indicate worry, anxiety or even depression.'

When the great man had left, the teacher asked the child, 'Tommy, why did you draw everything in black?'

'Please miss,' he said, 'I couldn't get the tops off the other colours.'

Let The Rabbits Run

Imagine there is a meadow. In that meadow there is a duck, a fish, an eagle, a squirrel and a rabbit. They decide they want to have a school so they can be clever just like people.

With the help of some grown-up animals, they come up with a curriculum they believe will make a well-rounded animal:

Running
Swimming
Tree-climbing
Jumping
And ... flying.

On the first day of school, Brer Rabbit combed his ears and went off to his running class. There he was a star. He ran to the top of the hill and back as fast as he could go, and oh, didn't it feel good!

The next class was swimming. When the rabbit smelt the chlorine he said, 'Wait a minute! Rabbits don't like to swim.'

The instructor said, 'Well, you may not like it now, but five years from now you'll know it was a good thing for you.'

In the tree-climbing lesson a tree trunk was set at a 30-degree angle, so all the animals had a chance to succeed. The little rabbit tried so hard he hurt his leg.

In the jumping lesson, the rabbit got along well: in the flying lesson, he had a problem. So, the teacher gave him a psychological test and discovered he belonged in remedial flying.

The next morning, he went on to his swimming lesson. The instructor said, 'Today we jump into the water.'

'Wait, wait. I talked to my parents about swimming. They didn't learn to swim. We don't like to get wet. I'd like to stop this course.'

The instructor said, 'You can't stop it now. At this point you have a choice: either you jump in, or you fail.'

The rabbit jumped in. He panicked! He went down once. He went down twice. Bubbles came up. The instructor saw that he was drowning and pulled him out. The other animals had never seen anything quite as funny as this wet rabbit who looked more like a rat without a tail, and so they chirped and jumped and barked and laughed at the rabbit. The rabbit was more humiliated than he had ever been in his life. He wanted desperately to get out of the lesson that day. He was glad when it was over.

He thought he would head for home; that his parents would understand and help him. When he arrived, he said to his parents, 'I don't like school. I just want to be free.'

'If rabbits are going to get ahead, you have to get a diploma,' replied his parents.

The rabbit said, 'I don't want a diploma.'

The parents said, 'You're going to get a diploma whether you like it or not.'

They argued and finally the parents made the rabbit go to bed. In the morning the rabbit headed off for school with a slow hop. Then he remembered that the head teacher had said that any time he had a problem he should remember that the school counsellor's door is always open.

When he arrived at school, he hopped up in the chair by the school counsellor and said, 'I don't like school.'

And the school counsellor said, 'Mmmm – tell me about it.'

And the rabbit did.

The school counsellor said, 'Rabbit, I hear you. I hear you say that you don't like school because you don't like swimming. I think I have diagnosed that correctly. Rabbit, I tell you what we'll do. You're doing well in running. I don't know why you need to work on running. I'll arrange it so you don't have to go running anymore; you can have two periods of swimming instead.'

When the rabbit heard that, he was very upset!

As the rabbit hopped out of the school counsellor's office he looked up and saw his friend the wise old owl, who cocked his head and said, 'Brer Rabbit, life doesn't have to be this way. We could have schools and businesses where people are allowed to concentrate on what they do well.'

Brer Rabbit was inspired. He thought that when he graduated, he would start a business where the rabbits would do nothing but run, the squirrels could just climb trees, and the fish could just swim. As he disappeared into the meadow, he sighed softly to himself and said, 'Oh my, what a great place that would be.'[5]

Brothers

Two little boys, aged eight and ten, are excessively mischievous. They are always getting into trouble and their parents know all about it. If any mischief occurs in their town, the two boys are probably involved.

The boys' mother heard that a local clergyman had been successful in helping children with behavioural issues, so she asked if he would speak with her boys. The clergyman agreed, but he asked to see them individually. It was decided that the younger brother would see him first.

The clergyman, a huge man with a booming voice, sat the younger boy down. He was determined to convince the child that God was everywhere and could therefore see everything. He asked him sternly, 'Do you know where God is, son?' The boy's mouth dropped open, but he made no response, sitting there wide-eyed with his mouth hanging open. So the clergyman repeated the question in an even sterner tone, 'Where is God?!' Again, the boy made no attempt to answer. The preacher raised his voice even more and shook his finger in the boy's face and bellowed, 'Where is God?!' The boy screamed and bolted from the room. He ran directly home. The older brother was about to go for his session when he found his sibling hiding in his wardrobe. He said, 'What's wrong?' The little boy, gasping for breath, replied, 'Don't go and see him. We are in BIG trouble. God is missing, and they think we did it!'

The Things We've Handed Down

I have found that there's no rhyme or reason to the things that are handed down to the generations that come behind us.

Of course, it's no surprise that a child of a skilled baker may themselves, after many hours of help, become a great baker themselves. Or that the child of a world class footballer learns some skills from their mother or father. It's not these things that intrigue me though. What I find fascinating is the child whose mannerisms are just like their uncle's, or the child who has the same nose as countless others in his bloodline. I love seeing bits of Rob and I in our children and grandchildren (well, the good bits at least!) and often wonder what of us will be found in the generations to come.

I came across a song which summed up the thoughts that I've had looking at my own children and grandchildren.

One of my favourite songs is Marc Cohn's 'The Things We've Handed Down' in which he expresses many of the same thoughts that I've had looking at my own children and grandchildren. Like hand-me-down clothes, family traits and characteristics can so often (and sometimes startlingly!) crop up in the next generation. The question is – what things are we handing down?

Tokens Of Love

You may already know the story of Helen Keller, but in case you don't, allow me to share it with you.

When she was a toddler, Helen contracted a disease which left her both blind and deaf. She learnt Braille and a method known as Tadoma, in which placing hands on a person's face – touching their lips, throat, jaw and nose – are used to feel vibrations and movements that are associated with speaking. She actually learned to communicate by holding her fingers against her tutor's larynx. Helen graduated from Cambridge College Massachusetts, toured the world lecturing, and founded the Helen Keller Home for blind children. One day a journalist said to her, 'Miss Keller, can you imagine anything worse than being blind?'

'Oh yes,' said Helen. 'To be able to see and have no vision.'

I just love that mindset.

The above account is well known but what is not so well known is the story of Helen Keller and the inventor Alexander Graham Bell. He set up a trust for her to attend college – an inventor and a young blind and deaf child became friends. It was through that relationship that Helen Keller became the first unsighted deaf person to earn a Bachelor of Arts degree. She once wrote to Bell and said, 'You have been and are very good to me, and so is Mrs Bell, and though I be silent, I cherish ever the many tokens of your love.'[6]

I love the phrase, 'the many tokens of your love.' Yes, it's a little quaint, but so very profound. A very obvious token was the payment of the college fees, but Alexander and his wife had clearly given many others too. Over time they had impacted Helen's life, not just through the big gesture, but more importantly, through the many, consistent 'tokens of love' in smaller, everyday things. Like an encouraging message, a thoughtful card – a simple act of kindness.

I suppose that when they gave those 'tokens', they had no idea of the woman Helen would become and the many lives she would change.

Unspoken Grief

I can still clearly remember the night, many years ago, when it happened.

It was late and Rob and I were watching television. I suddenly had a great need for the loo. When I got to the bathroom, I realised straight away that I was having a miscarriage. I made my way back to Rob, shaking and very tearful. We rushed to the hospital. When we got there, they were so kind, but all the beds in the maternity ward were full and after my operation I was given a place in a geriatric ward. I remember Rob and I holding hands in the darkness of the early morning and crying while elderly people slept fitfully around us.

As the morning light peeked through the curtains, I woke to see a hospital worker at the end of my bed asking me why I was in the geriatric ward – perhaps they'd had a stressful night and although the staff had been wonderful, I felt little compassion from this person. My heart felt so heavy. Thankfully, a few moments later a lovely Catholic priest came and sat by my bed. He talked with me, showed me such compassion and offered to pray with me before he moved on to the next patient. I have never forgotten the kindness he showed me in the most difficult of times.

Those who have experienced a miscarriage will know too well not only the loss and grief that you feel at this time, but also the guilt, emptiness, fear and even the deep sense of loneliness that can rear their heads too. A miscarriage is a dreadful shock – physically, emotionally and spiritually – and can bring with it so many questions. Miscarriages rarely occur because of something that the mother did or didn't do. And yet it can be so easy to blame ourselves. I can remember feeling overwhelming emptiness and loss for a long time after we lost our baby.

It's so important that we recognise the complicated thoughts, feelings and emotions that can come following the loss of a child. One of these is jealousy. It's incredibly difficult to watch somebody else's dreams come true when yours have just been shattered. To see friends announce pregnancies and births when you've been through the most horrific loss is so very hard. I learnt that I needed to give myself some grace, especially on those tough days, and remember that my feelings were understandable and normal.

The loss of a baby can put an enormous strain on a couple's relationship – it certainly did on ours. Not everyone finds it easy to express their feelings and for those of us who find talking about how we feel difficult, bickering and arguments can easily become the norm. I learnt that there is no shame or weakness in asking for help to get ourselves and our relationship back on track.

Of course, friends and family are often kind, but when you have not been through this experience, it is very easy to underestimate the incredible trauma that often comes with miscarriage. I remember people saying those two fatal words that are often uttered after a bereavement: 'At least.'

'At least you're young – you can have more children.'

'At least you have each other.'

'At least you have faith in God.'

I wanted to say to them, 'All those things are wonderfully true. But I wanted that baby. Don't try to give me answers, defend God, or rationalise my pain. Just be there for us.'

Seeing In The Dark

*Hope is being able to see
that there is light
despite all the darkness.*

Desmond Tutu

Note To Self

Don't sit on the floor without a
plan for how to get up!

Is The Glass Half Full Or ...?

A family had twin boys whose only resemblance to each other was their looks. If one felt it was too hot, the other thought it was too cold. If one said the TV was too loud, the other claimed the volume needed to be turned up. Opposite in every way, one was an eternal optimist, the other a doom and gloom pessimist.

Just to see what would happen, on Christmas Day their father loaded the pessimist's room with every imaginable toy and game. The optimist's room he loaded with horse hay.

That night the father passed by the pessimist's room and found him sitting amid his new gifts crying bitterly.

'Why are you crying?' the father asked.

'Because my friends will be jealous, I'll have to read all these instructions before I can do anything with this stuff, I'll constantly need batteries, and my toys will eventually get broken.' answered the pessimist twin.

Passing the optimist twin's room, the father found him dancing for joy in the piles of hay. 'What are you so happy about?' he asked.

The boy replied, 'There's got to be a pony in here somewhere!'

Just recently, I came across a wonderful definition that sums it up: An optimist is someone who figures out that taking a step backward after taking a step forward is not a disaster, it's a cha-cha.

Making A Difference

Here's a confession: I love talking. I've even caught myself talking to our neighbour's cat! I know that lots of people find it hard to start a conversation out of nowhere, but in my experience it's almost always worth it. I've often found that a small 'hello' can turn into a wonderful conversation that makes someone's day. The mighty power of the smallest of words can make someone feel seen. I remember smiling at an elderly lady in a supermarket. She thanked me and said, 'It's so nice to be noticed.' I wonder how often she felt noticed and I'm glad that my smile made a difference to her. It cost me nothing but meant the world to her.

I remember being on a plane and watching a young mum try to cope with three little ones on her own. They weren't being naughty, but they were being kids – noisy. She was doing her very best to keep them occupied, but the stares of disapproval she was getting from some of the other passengers were causing her to become increasingly flustered. As she was getting off the plane, laden with books, crayons, toys and a small baby, I whispered to her, 'I think you're an incredible mum.' She looked at me, blinking away tears, and said, 'Thank you. You have no idea how much I needed that.'

There is so much need all around us. Someone once said, 'Everyone we meet is fighting an inner battle we know nothing about'. How true that is. I know that I've definitely walked around with a smile on my face, pretending that everything's OK and masking what's really going on inside. If we went about our daily lives assuming that we needed to be gentle and show extra kindness to every person we meet, I wonder what the world would look like.

Some time ago, I was queuing at the tills of our local Aldi. I got chatting to the lady behind me and she shared some of her life with me. She was a nurse and had worked through the entire Covid pandemic. She told me that she'd worked so many hours and was feeling totally exhausted – physically and emotionally. After paying for my shopping and bagging it up, a sudden thought hit me. I had bought myself a bunch of flowers but realised that the lovely nurse behind me needed them more than I did. As I handed them to her, she burst into tears. This small gesture obviously meant a lot to her but of course acts of kindness are not just one-way affairs, and as I left the shop I was smiling.

I remember watching a film called *Pay it Forward*. It was about a young boy who decided that instead of returning a favour, he would pay it forward by doing good deeds for three new people. This film reminded me of an occasion where Rob and I drove over the Severn Bridge connecting England and Wales. At that time there was a toll charge. We drew up to the toll booth and were surprised to be told by the attendant that the people in the car ahead of us (who were complete strangers to us) had paid our fee. What a lovely surprise and a challenge for us to then 'pay it forward' to someone else.

What We Pass On

Being a grandparent is one of the greatest privileges I've ever had. It can be fun and challenging, and my brain is constantly stretched by all my grandkids' amazing questions (many of which I cannot answer, especially if they are about maths!) Last Christmas we all went out for hot chocolate. Some of them wanted to donate their pocket money towards the final bill as they felt that maybe I was a little too old to pay for it all myself! Before we set off, we all decided to spray our hair with a small streak of blue dye (one that washed out, of course, otherwise their parents would have disowned me!) The grandkids thought it was so much fun, a little naughty and a bit outrageous too!

Grandparents are the keepers of family stories. I still have the memories of my Nan telling me stories when I wasn't well and home from school. She would tell me of her childhood and the time that she spent with her grandparents, and so the stories have been passed down the generations. When children hear family stories, it helps them know who they are and where they have come from. Their confidence is built, and they're given a sense of belonging. But unless someone in the family keeps the stories going, they'll be lost forever. I hope that my grandchildren will one day tell their own grandchildren stories about me.

There are some creative ways that family stories and memories can be passed down:

— Write a history of your family.

— Put together a scrapbook.

— Make a picture gallery of aunts, uncles, grandparents etc.

— Create a family tree and let the children in your family draw some pictures to go with them.

— Tell them about their own parents when they were young.

I often wonder about the kind of adults that my grandchildren will grow up to be, and so I have made a commitment to pray for them each day. I also want to support them for as long as I can. I want to be there as a safe person that they can talk to and share their plans and secrets with. I want to, along with their parents, encourage them in their dreams and support them in the heartaches.

Whatever family looks like for you, passing stories from one generation to the next can be a great way to bring people together and connect them for years to come.

Make The Time

Do you ever find yourself halfway through the year wondering how we're now closer to next Christmas than last Christmas? I do – regularly! None of us know how much time we have on this earth. We need to make the most of every moment. I think that this poem captures that perfectly…

Every minute someone leaves this world behind.
Age has nothing to do with it.
We are all in this line without realising it.
We never know how many people are before us.
We cannot move to the back of the line.
We cannot step out of the line.
We cannot avoid the line.
So, while we wait in the line:
Make moments count.
Make a difference.
Make that call.
Make priorities.
Make the time.
Make your gifts known.
Make a nobody feel a somebody.
Make your voice heard.
Make someone smile.
Make the change.
Make up.
Make peace.
Make sure you tell your people they are loved.
Make waves.
Make sure you have no regrets.
Make sure you are ready.
This world will often leave you wishing you had just five
more minutes.
If you can, wake up each day and realise it is a gift.

Attributed to Marianne Baum

What tokens of your love can you give to someone else today?

(Tokens Of Love)

What areas of
your life do you
need to search for
light in?

(Seeing In
The Dark)

Which brother do you relate to most? Are you an optimist or a pessimist?

(Is The Glass Half Full Or …?)

How can you make someone's world a little brighter today?
(Making A Difference)

89

What one
practical thing
can you do to
make the most of
every moment?

(Make The Time)

Letting Go

I hear people complain that as we get older our memories fail. This is of course true, but there is sometimes the problem of not being able to forget. What of those occasions when we have known great hurt? Time and time again people say to me, 'I've forgiven them, but I simply can't forget – I wish I could.'

Perhaps we can't erase those memories. But as an act of the will, we can choose not to nurse them, but rather, year by year, gradually let them go. And what of the wrongs that we have done? For that, we need more. We need to discover somebody who can forgive – and really can forget.

'For I will forgive … and will remember their sins no more.'
– Hebrews 8:12

Thank God for that.

Chased By Time

When we'd been married for a just a few years Rob and I were walking along a pier and in front of us were an elderly couple. As they walked, they held hands. I nudged Rob and said, 'That will be us one day.' Not long ago, we were walking along together holding hands and we turned at the sound of somebody giggling. It was a young couple …

What's With The Fork?

I heard a story about a lady in America. She was very near the end of her life and asked her pastor to come to her house to discuss the details of her funeral. She had written out which hymns she wanted sung, some Bible readings, and the names of people that she'd like to take part.

As the pastor was about to leave, she said, 'Oh, and one more thing. I like to maintain the tradition in our family of having the coffin open so people can walk past and say a final goodbye.' The pastor agreed that would be fine. And then she said, 'I'd like you to place this in my right hand.' She handed him her favourite dog-eared Bible. 'And in my left hand please place a fork.' The pastor looked puzzled and asked, 'Why a fork?' The old lady smiled, 'When I was a child at church potluck dinners, I remember that when the dishes were being cleared after the main course, people would sometimes say, "Keep your fork." I loved it when they said that, because it meant that something even better than the main meal was coming, like chocolate cake or deep-dish apple pie. As people pass my casket they will ask you, "What's with the fork?" And I'd like you to tell them, "Emily believed that the best is yet to come."'

Give Me A Light

I have just listened to King Charles III's first Christmas speech. I have never missed one of his mother's and I was deeply touched as he spoke.

At the start of 2023, I read again the poem that Queen Elizabeth's father, King George VI, quoted in his 1939 Christmas broadcast. In the book *The Servant Queen and the King She Serves*, which was published for Queen Elizabeth's 90th birthday, the Queen says that it was her, as a young princess of thirteen years old, who handed the poem to her father. It seems that the poem remained a source of comfort to the Queen Mother, and she had it engraved on stone plaques and fixed to the gates of The King George VI Memorial Chapel at Windsor Castle where the King was buried. The Queen Mother was also buried there and the words of 'The Gate of the Year' by Minnie Louise Haskins were included in a reflection in her funeral order of service.

Here is part of that poem:

> *And I said to the man who stood at*
> *the gate of the year:*
> *'Give me a light that I may tread*
> *safely into the unknown.'*
> *And he replied:*
> *'Go out into the darkness and put*
> *your hand into the Hand of God.*
> *That shall be to you better than light*
> *and safer than a known way.'*
> *So I went forth, and finding the Hand*
> *of God, trod gladly into the night.*
> *And He led me towards the hills and*
> *the breaking of day in the lone East.*
>
> **The Gate of the Year**
> **Minnie Louise Haskins**

The Choice

Just the other day I heard one of the grandkids say to their parents, 'It's not fair.' I wanted to take him in my arms and tell him that unfortunately that is true – not just about your brother going to bed a little later than you, but so often in the whole of life. There are no easy answers to the injustices that so often assail us, but how we deal with them will affect our lives forever. There are several times in my life when I have felt so hurt, I honestly felt I could never get over it. The following words that I came across were not the whole answer, but they were a very good start.

> *You either get bitter or you get better. It's that simple. You either take what has been dealt to you and allow it to make you a better person or you allow it to tear you down. The choice does not belong to fate; it belongs to you.*
>
> **Author unknown**

Be strong enough to
stand alone, smart
enough to know
when you need help
and brave enough to
ask for it.

New Beginnings

Dr Harold Bosley was the minister of Christ Church New York. He was once a member of a panel discussion at the University of Chicago. During question time somebody asked, 'Is there anything unique about Christianity?' On the same panel was a Jewish rabbi who asked if he might be permitted to answer the question first. This is what he said:

> 'The unique thing about Christianity is that it never gives anyone up. It always helps a man or woman begin again. There is always the possibility of a new start.'

When I was a child in primary school, I used to love it when the teachers gave us a brand-new exercise book. I used to open it and touch its pristine pages. All the old mistakes, blots and smudges were gone. And as I've got older, I have been grateful for things much more important than an exercise book – for the wonderful chance of a new beginning.

The Power Of A Seed

I often think back to my old Sunday School teachers. Miss Williams was tiny and had an infectious smile and giggle. Miss Lamarque was sterner, but I knew that she loved us. Mrs Harker was like a mother hen. Their names are not on any blue plaques outside their former homes; they received no honours from the Queen, and not one of them ever wrote a book. But they planted a seed in me. When I spoke at the Royal Albert Hall in front of three thousand women at the *To Change the Future* conference, those old Sunday school teachers were on my mind. I reminded us all that even tiny seeds are powerful and urged us not to despise small actions – we never know where they will end.

Somebody put it well:

> *'You can count the seeds in an orange, but you can't count the oranges in a seed.'*

That's A Mirror!

A woman was out with an old friend for lunch. As they were eating, she nudged her friend and pointed at two elderly women sat at a table, just the other side of a small wall in the restaurant. 'That will be us in a few years' time,' she giggled.

Her friend replied wearily. 'Sarah – that's a mirror.'

Be My Best Friend

I had ten minutes to stand in the playground waiting for my granddaughter Lily to come out of class. Most of the children were running around with an energy that took my breath away! As I stood, I watched with interest the interactions they had as they played games with each other. It was fascinating! Some stood on the sidelines looking lost, waiting to be asked to join in.

Some days later I asked a young girl the name of her best friend at school. She thought for a moment and then replied, 'Well, some days it's Amy and other days it's Alice.' Sometimes I've felt like that about some of my friends – but lacked that little girl's candour!

That evening I thought long and hard about my friends both past and present. My mind went back to when I was in high school. Jackie and I were inseparable. Through the long summer holidays, we would spend most of our time together. I remember walking around the local park constantly chatting to her, while looking out for the 'local talent', and then running a mile if the boys came over to talk. During those years she was like my second skin, but sadly at the end of our school life together we just drifted apart. I sometimes ask myself what happened to that friendship we had. We laughed and cried together and told each other our deepest secrets. I guess our lives changed as we grew up and of course some friendships, like life itself, have seasons.

And perhaps, even with deep friendships, it's not longevity that is most important. I read a lovely quote recently 'Friendship isn't about who you've known the longest – it's about someone who walked into your life and said, "I'm here for you" – and proved it'. I like that. I believe a true friend is someone with whom you don't have to pretend to be anyone or anything. Of course, they might like you to change in some ways, and yes, at times you may let each other down but they are 'for you' – whatever.

And, of course, in a close friendship it's not all one-way. A true friend will help you in times of need, but they will allow you to help them too. It's hard to get close to somebody who would climb Everest to rescue you but would never dream of asking for help themselves.

In his book *Applauding the Strugglers*, Jim McGuiggan recounts a story about the novelist Marjorie Byrd. On a visit to her friend in the Western Highlands of Scotland, the two of them experienced a gale. At the height of the fierce storm there was a knock on the door. A family friend, a young lad who because of a disability had great difficulty in walking, had walked all the way from a nearby village to check on Mrs MacIntosh. He arrived soaked to the skin. She brought him in to warm by the fire and Marjorie Byrd commented on the howling storm. The boy said, 'Aren't you afraid?' The novelist was about to say no when Mrs MacIntosh interrupted quickly. 'Of course we were afraid, but now you're here it's all right.' The boy straightened his twisted frame and said, 'Well, then I'd best be checking to make sure everything is snug.'

There's research to show what an incredible effect good friendships can have. According to one study, having just two or three close friends can affect our physical and mental health positively – and even cause us to live longer! But life is busy, and friendships take work. Sometimes I have to make myself make that call or send that message.

'Hi – it's Di here. It's been too long. Do you have time for coffee?'

Oh Joy!

I recently read a story in the *London Times* that will surely bring a smile to the face of every hassled mother. It reported that Marie Kondo, the guru of tidiness, whose book on the subject sold three million copies, has eased up on the tidying ideas since she has given birth to her third child. I confess to having felt some satisfaction as I read it. My children learnt to spell in the dust in my home. I would say, 'Write your name in the dust on the coffee table. That's good. Now rub it out.' By the time the poor child had worked her way around all the furniture the house was spotless.

Many years ago, I came across a piece entitled 'Are you ready to have children?'

Women: to prepare for maternity, put on a dressing gown and stick a beanbag down the front. Leave it there for nine months. After nine months take out 10% of the beans. Men: to prepare for paternity, go to the local chemist, tip the contents of your wallet on the counter, and tell the pharmacist to help himself. Then go to the supermarket. Arrange to have your salary paid directly to their head office. Go home. Pick up the paper. Read it for the last time.

Can you stand the mess that children make? To find out, first smear Marmite on to the sofa and jam onto the curtains. Hide a fish finger behind the stereo and leave it there all summer. Stick your fingers in the flowerbeds then rub them on the clean walls. Cover the stains with crayon. How does that look?

Hollow out a melon. Make a small hole in the side. Suspend it from the ceiling and swing it from side to side. Now get a bowl of soggy Weetabix and attempt to spoon it into the swaying melon by pretending to be an aeroplane. Continue until half the Weetabix is gone. Tip the rest into your lap, making sure that a lot of it falls on the floor.

You are now ready to feed a twelve-month-old baby.[7]

But hey, Marie, don't feel too bad about giving up tidying for a while. Most of us mothers were amazed you lasted until your third!

People We Remember

The American memoirist and civil rights activist Maya Angelou said, 'I've learned that people will forget what you said, people will forget what you did, but they will never forget how you made them feel.'

There is a story about Jennie Jerome, Winston Churchill's mother, who dined two consecutive nights with former British prime ministers. The first night was spent with Gladstone and the following night with Disraeli. She was asked what the difference was. She said, 'When I left the dining room after sitting next to Gladstone, I thought he was the cleverest man in England. But when I sat next to Disraeli, I left feeling that I was the cleverest woman.'

Disraeli had shown an interest in her life, asked many questions and listened. How wise it is to listen! After all, as someone once put it, 'Nobody ever learned anything new by hearing themselves speak.'

The Time Of Our Life

We say to ourselves, 'If only I had more time', but of course, each of us has all the time there is. I think this poem sums it up.

And so, all men run after time, Lord.
They pass through life running – hurried, jostled,
overburdened, frantic – and they never get there.
They haven't time.
In spite of all their efforts, they're still short of time,
of a great deal of time.
Lord, you must have made a mistake in your calculations –
there is a big mistake somewhere.
The hours are too short,
The days are too short
Our lives are too short.
You who are beyond time,
Lord, you smile to see us fighting it.
And you know what you are doing.
You make no mistakes in your distribution of time to men.
You give each one time to do what you want him to do.
But we must not lose time, waste time, kill time,
For time is a gift that you give us
But a perishable gift
A gift that does not keep.
Lord, I have time
I have plenty of time
All the time that you give me.
The years of my life

The days of my years
The hours of my day
They are all mine
Mine to fill quietly, calmly
But to fill completely up to the brim
To offer them to you, that of their insipid water,
You may make a rich wine such as you made once in Cana of
Galilee.
I am not asking you tonight, Lord,
for time to do this and then that
But for your grace to do conscientiously in the time that you
give me what you want me to do.

Michel Quoist (1918-1997) Prayers of Life.

What things do you need to gradually let go of?

(Letting Go)

What good
things are you
most looking
forward to?

(What's With
The Fork?)

What situations are you facing at the moment that have the power to make you bitter or better? What choice will you make?

(The Choice)

What seeds can
you plant in those
around you?
(The Power Of
A Seed)

117

Who could you
reach out to
this week?

(Be My Best
Friend)

Fake Or Fortune

I'm sure that many of you are talented at music or art, but I'm afraid that for me, that is a high-reaching dream! I can tinkle on the piano, but it wouldn't be something that Bach or Handel would be appreciative of. I can just about draw a vaguely recognisable house or cat, but a masterpiece it certainly won't be. This hasn't stopped me from hoping though, or imagining a painting of mine on the living room wall … well, there's no harm in dreaming, is there?

During one of the Covid-19 lockdowns, I decided to buy myself some watercolour paints and try yet again to fulfil the artistic potential that I'm sure I have hidden somewhere within me. My friends were very encouraging, bless them, although I did need to correct the way they were holding my first picture after they'd turned it around a few times trying to make sense of it! I thought it all rather unfair. I have often looked at highly acclaimed modern art worth millions of pounds and found that I really couldn't connect with it at all. So, what is the difference between those paintings and mine?

Would-be artist that I am, I love watching the TV programme *Fake or Fortune*. My second thought after I'd seen the first episode was how much I would love to have the presenter Fiona Bruce's job. (My first thought was how much I'd love to have Fiona Bruce's figure.) Imagine travelling to different parts of the world and meeting with all kinds of people. Imagine going into their homes and looking around to try and discover what kind of people they are, the sorts of things they like to collect, and whether they are tidy or messy or have coffee rings on the coffee table. Yes, I would certainly fit into that role very nicely. But, of course, the programme's focus is on art, not people – and when it came to discovering whether someone's piece of art is worth a fortune or not, I would be totally stumped.

Oh, I can pick out a Lowry matchstick people picture, but whether it was genuine or not is a different question. Nonetheless, I still love the programme. You're taken into a fascinating world of discovery, walking you through the fine details of the picture and the life of the artist. Along with the owners, I'm on tenterhooks, waiting to discover the answer – is the painting real or fake? Hearing the outcome, either way, can be very emotional.

Sometimes, I feel a little like one of those pieces of art and, like the experts, I am still trying to discover the real me. I know that we all do it, but sometimes I feel that the Dianne people think they are seeing isn't the real person at all. And I wonder what people would think if they knew the real me.

It took me a long time to realise that unlike the presenters on the TV show, who have to peel away the outer layers to find the real thing, God knows exactly who I am. He knows me inside and out, and I can't fool him like I can sometimes fool the world. The amazing thing is that he loves me simply for who I am. I don't have to pretend to be someone else; there is nothing to hide or cover up. God knows the worst about me, but he loves me anyway. I dare not take him for granted: Max Lucado echoes the popular saying: 'It is true that God loves us as we are, but he loves us too much to leave us as we are.' I am precious in his sight. Perhaps sometimes a fake – but always, in his eyes at least – worth a fortune.

Isn't it amazing —
I hang something
up in my wardrobe
for a while and
when I go back to
it, it's shrunk
two sizes!

The Big Decision

Sometimes I come across something that challenges me deeply. When I first read this, I thought to myself, 'Such a positive attitude is impossible for most of us.' Nevertheless, this woman's spirit inspires me to change.

This 92-year-old petite, well-poised and proud lady, who is fully dressed each morning by eight o'clock, with her hair fashionably coiffed and makeup perfectly applied moved to a nursing home today.

Her husband of 70 years passed away, making the move necessary. After many hours of waiting patiently in the lobby of the nursing home, she smiled sweetly when told her room was ready. As she manoeuvred her walker to the elevator, the carer provided a visual description of her tiny room, including the eyelet sheets that had been hung on her window. 'I love it,' she stated with the enthusiasm of an eight-year-old having just been presented with a new puppy.

'Mrs. Jones, you haven't seen the room yet … just wait.'

'That doesn't have anything to do with it,' she replied. 'Happiness is something you decide on ahead of time. Whether I like my room or not doesn't depend on how the furniture is arranged. It's how I arrange my mind. I already decided to love it. It's a decision I make every morning when I wake up. I have a choice. I can spend the day in bed recounting the difficulty I have with the parts of my body that no longer work or get out of bed and be thankful for the ones that do. Each day is a gift, and as long as my eyes open, I'll focus on the new day and all the happy memories I have stored away just for this time in my life. Old age is like a bank account. You withdraw from what you've put in. So, my advice to you would be to deposit a lot of happiness in the bank account of memories. And thank you for your part in filling my memory bank. I am still depositing.'

Looking Back

One of the most scenic routes in Scotland is along the edge of Loch Long. At the end of a steep climb the traveller can enjoy spectacular views of Glencoe and the Arrochar Alps. This wonderful place gets its name from the stone set at the summit: 'Rest and be Thankful'. As I thought about that unusual name it challenged me to take time, to stop from all the hurry for a moment and simply be grateful.

In *The Pilgrim's Progress*, John Bunyan's classic account of Christian's journey to the heavenly city, we read of the trail from the City of Destruction, through the Slough of Despond, the Valley of Humiliation and the Valley of the Shadow of Death. But then Christian and his fellow pilgrims arrive at the River of the Water. There they find a beautiful meadow, filled with lilies and green all year round. The meadow was a safe place for them to lie down and sleep and provided them with fruit to eat and water to drink. Fed, watered and rested, they sang.

It is true that they had experienced many trials and hardships, but this was a moment to stop and rest and perhaps reflect. There are many challenges, but just now I take a moment to look back on the distance come, and the many blessings along the way.

Today, I take a moment to rest and be thankful.

The Indelible Print

Many of us will have people that we're teaching, mentoring, or encouraging in life. Some may be people that we've journeyed with for many years, while others may be walking with us for just a season. I like this quote about the impact we can have on people as they find their own path:

> 'You will teach them to fly, but they will not fly your flight. You will teach them to dream, but they will not dream your dream. You will teach them to live, but they will not live your life. Nevertheless, in every flight, in every life, in every dream, the print of the way you taught them will remain.'

> **Source unknown**

Don't compare
your Chapter One
to someone else's
Chapter Twenty.

The Letter

It was a sunny but cold October morning and I'd just driven to the local supermarket car park. No, not for grocery shopping – for a mammogram. The huge 'caravan' these things take place in make it oh-so-obvious to anyone (usually quite a few people in a supermarket car park) why you are going up the steps.

When I came out, the sun had gone in, and the rain was falling fast and furious. But all was well, as I was meeting a friend in a local coffee shop. The only problem was that the cakes on the counter were irresistible. I managed to withstand temptation – for half an hour. I was quite proud that I lasted that long! The shop had a gift section, and after our refreshments we had a wander round. Already the Christmas bits and pieces were out. I know it was really too early, but I loved it. I love planning for Christmas, especially for the grandkids – my dream job would be to be Santa's helper.

A few weeks later, I was out and about again, this time popping to a small shopping area near my house. I guess I could have walked there – if I had, there would have been a far better outcome to this part of the story. While I was reversing into a parking spot, a car was also backing out and bumped into me. I got out, as did the other driver, a very sweet younger woman, and we both apologised. All was settled amicably – we agreed that everything would go through the insurance.

When I got home, I broke the news to Rob that I'd banged the car. Rob doesn't make a fuss over those kinds of things, but I was cross with myself. And then I saw an unopened letter addressed to me on the kitchen worktop. I tore it open and scanned it. I was being called back for another mammogram. I knew that fewer than one in ten women who are recalled are found to have cancer; nevertheless, my concerns and worries changed in a millisecond. That dent in the back of my car was now way down the list.

The appointment was in two weeks' time, and Rob came with me. I think the worst part of it was waiting in the reception. I am always fascinated by people in places like dentists' or doctors' waiting rooms – I've even had the giggles at the vets. Watching a couple of dogs growling at some cats once, I think I almost saw the owners start to growl at each other. I did a double take another time when a very large lizard slid down a young boy's shoulder. But here in the breast clinic it was different; it was incredibly quiet.

My name was called, and everyone looked up and stared at me sombrely. I was ushered to a cubicle to take my top clothes off and told to put on what looked like a small poncho. Then I went into a waiting room where about a dozen other women sat, all wearing the same colour poncho. I couldn't help it – I found myself saying: 'We look like we're in some kind of pop group.' A few women smiled; the others looked at me as though I had just landed from another planet.

After the repeat mammogram, I was called in to see the consultant. Rob was able to come with me and we sat looking intently at the man who was about to tell me something that could change my life. I remember the nurse who was with him gave me such a lovely smile, and then the doctor told me as gently as he could that I did have a lump. My mind went blank, and I felt the room closing in on me. It turned out that the lump was cancerous, and I needed an operation. I don't very often find it hard to talk, but I did on this occasion.

Christmas came and went and the day for my operation was upon me. I surprised myself with how calm I was, and it was a great help to know that a group of friends and my family were praying for me. There were about seven of us in the ward and it didn't take long before we were talking. We each knew why we were there, so we were all on common ground, but I find it really interesting that on the whole, women do seem to gel so quickly under such circumstances. Even Rob noticed how soon we were chatting.

Following the operation, there were three weeks of radiotherapy. The staff there were amazing. By the time I rang the big bell which tells the other patients you've finished your treatment, everyone felt almost like family. I have kept in touch with one or two of the women I was in hospital with. We haven't been able to meet as often as we'd have liked, but that's where social media has come into its own. Never underestimate the difference that the support of family and friends can make when you're facing challenging times. We weren't made to do this life alone.

As I reflect on the very challenging period of my life, there is one thing that really sticks out in my mind. It is that incredible sense of community I felt with the other women in the ward, how quickly we bonded and the sheer power of not always having to be strong, but able to share fears as well as hopes. Some time ago I came across this incredible quote:

'If you want acquaintances, tell them your successes, but if you want friends, tell them your fears.'

A theologian was once asked for some advice on living the life of faith. He said,

'There are only two rules:
Rule 1: Go to Jesus.
Rule 2: Repeat rule 1.'

From Me To You
– A Letter From Long Ago

I recently came across a letter I wrote to our Care for the Family supporters almost twenty years ago. As I read again the words I had penned all those years ago, my mind went back down the decades …

The other day I said to Rob, 'How come you always write the letters to our Care for the Family supporters? Perhaps once in a while they'd like a couple of lines from me!' The second he agreed (and he did it a little too fast for my liking!), I regretted it. How would I start? How would I end? And most taxing of all – what would I put in the middle?

I've decided to simply tell you about three women who are on my mind at the moment in the hope that as you read you may feel some companionship with me, and perhaps with others that you know.

My friend is hurting. She is a wonderful mother, but her teenage daughter is breaking her heart. This girl seems determined to wreck her life and put her parents through unbelievable pain. One minute it's drugs, the next drink, and the other night this young woman was arrested. The cry that is always on my friend's lips is, 'Where did we go wrong?' I sit with her, and we drink coffee and cry together and I tell her she hasn't gone wrong anywhere. They have both been fantastic parents. But Rob and I are involved in Care for the Family –

we have shelves full of books, videos, and other resources on parenting in our headquarters – so why do I have no answers for her?

It is because there are no answers. I used to think that we didn't do 'no answers' – that there must be some advice, some tip, some book that can make things right. But as I've got older, I realise that sometimes you just have to be there for people in their pain, and together ask that God in his mercy come to our aid. The truth is, if I thought that in Care for the Family, we had to have answers to every situation that came across our path, I could not carry on. But I know that so often our role is simply to come alongside people, to 'put the coffee on' – even at a distance of hundreds of miles – and let people know they are not alone.

My mum has Alzheimer's. My bright, intelligent mother, who for all my life has counselled me, guided me and cared for me, can't recognise me when I visit. Oh, it's true that her eyes light up when I enter her room, but she doesn't know my name and seems intent on telling me about the imaginary characters that come in and out of her life these days. I miss drinking tea with her and laughing at real situations with her. I miss her wisdom. But more than all of that I simply miss her. But I am in my mid-fifties, and you would have every right to ask, 'If you can't get by without your mother now, when will you manage?' Perhaps you're right, but all I know is that it hurts. And at times alongside the hurt comes the guilt: why can't I do more for her? Did I make the best of all the years when her mind was clear? Am I a good daughter?

And yet there are wonderful moments. Before I leave her, I brush her hair and wipe the food from her lips. I straighten her dress and say, 'You look so pretty.' And then I always say, 'Jesus is with us, Mum.' And she smiles and replies, 'Yes, and He's the best.'

And finally, my daughter Katie. As I write she is approaching her first wedding anniversary. I could not love Paul, our son-in-law, more – he is God's gift to Kate (and us!) – But I still miss her. I live in a house of men – Rob, Lloyd, Ron (our guest of thirty years!) and Jezz the dog. When Rob wrote *Loving Against the Odds* almost fourteen years ago, he included a poem that I have often re-read as its truth came home to me.

> *She's gone.*
> *The child I once knew –*
> *and in her place –*
> *a woman*
> *vulnerable –*
> *lacking polish*
> *needing assurance perhaps*
> *but nevertheless*
> *a woman.*
> *The pain of her birth into womanhood*
> *was every bit as great as the pain of her birth*
> *the more so perhaps because of its suddenness*
> *then there were months of waiting*
> *of preparation*
> *now in a day –*
>
> *separation*
> *She's gone.*

She's gone
And I must let her go –
time now for painful rebuilding
where innocence – now knowledge
where wondering – now certainty
where hesitancy – now assurance
where once childlike trust
now I must accept a woman's vulnerability

Viewpoints considered – decisions made
– without me
ideas formulated carefully
girlhood pushed back
– womanhood embraced
But I will wait
Not in desperation – but patiently
for she may need me yet
as man needs man
and woman needs another woman –
and we will walk together, she and I
side by side.

For my child is gone
and in her place –
a woman.

(Previously unpublished poem, written by Susan Ashdown. Used with permission)

So, a mother, a widow and a young woman are on my mind just now. I think of them often, I pray for them most days. Their lives are intertwined with mine. But in my mind's eye I have other women. I see them now – thousands of them in our seminars. I remember them in ones and twos as they talk with me at the end of an event, I read their stories in a thousand letters. And with all my heart, as much as we can, I want Care for the Family to be there for each of them – sometimes with advice, often with answers, but at other moments just to say, 'Let us be with you as you go through this. We have sat with countless others through this experience – let theirs and our experiences bring you comfort and hope. You are not alone.'

The Winter Of My Life

Time has a way of moving quickly and catching you unawares with the passing years. It seems like only yesterday that I was a young woman, newly married and embarking on a new stage of life. And yet, somehow, it also feels like a lifetime ago and I find myself wondering where the years went.

But now it is the winter of my life, and that realisation often takes my breath away and catches me by surprise. I find myself pondering the things that I wanted to do and should have done while I had the chance. I catch myself reminiscing about the memories that I've made and the adventures that we've had so far. Great friends come to mind, as do the good and not so good times. It's all in a lifetime.

If you've read *You, Me and Coffee,* you'll know that in my kitchen I have a beautiful picture of my mum which was taken on our daughter Katie's wedding day. My mum is sat, in the winter of her life, between Katie and her husband Paul, and they are each kissing her on the cheek. This is an incredibly precious photo as my mum was unable to attend the wedding. At that time, she was in a nursing home suffering with Alzheimer's disease. My mum is sitting in her armchair, and she is roaring with laughter at the kisses that they've placed on her cheeks. When I look at this picture I smile because she is so happy, and cry because I miss her so much. She was such an incredible example to me. She lived her life caring not only for her family but for those around her too. She left a footprint for me that I try to follow as best I can. Yes, life is a precious gift – let's share it generously with those around us.

When she died, she wasn't able to leave us much money, but her legacy – not only of love but of kindness – is precious.

Before We Go

I can't believe that our time together has come to an end. I hope you've enjoyed reading this book as much as I have writing it. Although we haven't been able to sit down in person, I do hope that you feel like you've been able to get to know me a little better, as well as yourself through the journal pages, and perhaps grown a little closer to God too.

I'll leave you with this beautiful prayer from an unknown author I came across recently. I pray it for you with all my heart. Thank you for spending time with me.

May God be the light that shines on you.
May God be the star in your darkest night
And be your beacon of hope.
May God be the road on which you travel.
God be the earth that roots you.
May God be the rock where your home is built.
May God be the quiet stream where you find peace
God the fountain of refreshment
And God the source of inspiration.
May God be with you now and always.

Love, Di x

139

How can you remind yourself that you are precious in God's sight?

(Fake Or Fortune)

Take a moment to rest and be thankful. What are three things that you can be thankful for?

(Looking Back)

Who could your
words of kindness
make a difference
to this week?

(Words Of
Kindness)

What do you
want your
legacy to be?
(The Winter
Of My Life)

147

What one thing
will you take
away from this
journal?

(Before We Go)

150

Endnotes

1   William H. Davies, *Songs of Joy and Others* (London, 1911).

2   Dorothy L. Sayers, *Are Women Human? Astute and Witty Essays on the Role of Women in Society* (William B. Eerdmans Publishing Company, 2005).

3   Martin Moses, 'Remembering Kenyan Athlete Jacqueline Kiplimo Who Helped Athlete With Disability Quench His Thirst' Sports Brief, 25 March 2023, sportsbrief.com.

4   Jack Canfield, Mark Victor Hansen and Patty Hansen, *Condensed Chicken Soup for the Soul* (Hci, 1996).

5   Donald Clifton and Paula Nelson, *Play to your strengths: focus on what you do best and success will follow* (Piatkus, 1994).

6   Library of Congress, 'Letter from Helen Keller to Alexander Graham Bell, February 19, 1907'.

7   Colin Bowles, *The Beginner's Guide to Fatherhood* (HarperCollins Publishers Limited, 1992).

About Care For The Family

Established in 1988, Care for the Family is a charity based in the UK, but with an increasing reach internationally. Our aim is to support families whatever their circumstances. We provide this support, online and in person, for parents, couples and those who are bereaved, through events, courses, podcasts, volunteer befrienders, books and other evidence-based, accessible resources. We also train those who work with families whether in a professional or informal capacity.